Introduction

The purpose of this guide is to provide you, the Foreign Military Sales (FMS) customer, with a simplified overview of the process the United States (U.S.) uses to transfer defense articles and services from the U.S. to friendly foreign governments or to specific international organizations.

Nothing in this guide takes precedence over any U.S. Government (USG) regulations or formal policy guidance - including the Defense Security Cooperation Agency's (DSCA) Security Assistance Management Manual (SAMM), which is the most comprehensive source of information on policy and procedures.

The SAMM can be accessed at the following link: http://www.samm.dsca.mil.

Throughout this customer guide, we provide links to specific chapters within the SAMM and to other supporting documents. These links are in blue text and underlined to make them easier to identify as you read. Because the terminology used in Security Cooperation includes many acronyms, we'll start by providing you this link to the SAMM's List of Security Cooperation Acronyms and to the SAMM's Glossary of Terms so that you might look up any unfamiliar acronyms or terms.

Table of Contents

Security Cooperation Overview

The U.S. conducts Security Cooperation business with over 224 countries and international organizations around the world. We typically refer to specific Security Cooperation activities, such as sales of defense articles and services, as "programs" and conduct them under two primary U.S. legislative authorities: The Arms Export Control Act (AECA) (22 U.S.C. 2751 et seq.), as amended, and the Foreign Assistance Act of 1961 (FAA), as amended (22 U.S.C 2151 et seq.). Under these authorities, there are several options we may use to provide foreign partners with U.S. defense articles and services. The most commonly used option is Foreign Military Sales (FMS) - but we might also be able to meet your country's requirements using some of the other methods listed below. For any given purchase your country may be considering, there are benefits, limitations, and trade-offs associated with each of these options.

Foreign Military Sales (FMS)

FMS is a program that allows your government to purchase defense articles and services as well as design and construction services, from the USG. This program is operated on a "no-profit" and "no-loss" basis to the USG and requires an authorized representative from your government to submit a Letter of Request (LOR) to the USG for the desired defense articles and services.

Under FMS, the U.S. Department of Defense (DoD) procures defense articles and services for your country using the same acquisition process used to procure for its own military needs. This acquisition process is governed by the Federal Acquisition Regulation (FAR) and the Defense Federal Acquisition Regulation Supplement (DFARS). You, the foreign purchaser, benefit from U.S. DoD technical and operational expertise, procurement infrastructure, and purchasing practices. Your country also benefits from the lower unit costs that result when the U.S. DoD is able to combine your purchase with one of its own to achieve greater economy of scale. In addition, the U.S. DoD ensures your purchase takes into consideration all of the necessary training, support, and sustainment to give you the lasting operational capability you seek. We call this the "Total Package Approach". Finally, a major FMS program increases your country's interoperability with U.S. military forces, creating potential opportunities for joint training, joint exercises, cooperation in humanitarian assistance and disaster relief, and peacekeeping operations.

FMS requires a government-to-government agreement, known as a Letter of Offer and Acceptance (LOA) and sometimes referred to as an "FMS case". When your U.S. counterparts speak of "writing a case", they are talking about drafting an LOA. The LOA is written by the USG and must be formally accepted by your government. The LOA specifies the items and services to be provided to your country and an estimated cost and timeframe for doing so. The USG may supply items from its own stocks or it may establish a contract with a defense contractor to obtain the items on your behalf. Any contracts with U.S. defense contractors, if needed, will be written by the USG using standard USG competitive contracting procedures, to include robust oversight and auditing. The contract will be between the USG and the U.S. defense contractor. The USG then provides the equipment or service to your country as agreed in the government-to-government LOA. FMS customers are not legal participants in the procurement contract.

By U.S. law, the USG may neither make a profit from an FMS sale to your country nor take a loss. The LOA will require that your country pay the full cost associated with the FMS sale - which includes the cost of the defense equipment/services and any costs incurred by the USG while providing you with the defense equipment/services. We must ensure that, when the equipment or service is delivered and the case is closed, the USG has neither made a profit nor passed a debt to the U.S. taxpayer.

To build and re-build the administrative infrastructure necessary to support individual FMS cases would be a slow process and very costly to our foreign partners. Therefore, the USG maintains a standing infrastructure at the DoD level, within each of the Military Departments (MILDEPs), and within select other DoD organizations that conduct FMS. That standing infrastructure - skilled employees, information technology systems, offices, etc. - is funded by a 3.5% administrative surcharge applied to every FMS case. The FMS administrative surcharge fund is managed by the Defense Security Cooperation Agency (DSCA) under the oversight of the DoD Comptroller.

For additional general information on the FMS process, see SAMM Chapter 4.

Direct Commercial Sale (DCS)

DCS involves commercial contracts negotiated directly between your country and a U.S. defense contractor. DCS agreements are not administered by the USG and do not involve a government-to-government agreement. Instead, you deal with the U.S. contractor and that contractor is responsible for obtaining an export license from the Office of Defense Trade Controls, within the U.S. Department of State, to conduct each sale. The regulations for DCS are contained in the U.S. International Traffic in Arms Regulations (ITAR).

DCS is sometimes selected as an alternative to FMS when: a purchasing government's military requirements are significantly different from standard U.S. configurations; a purchasing government has a sufficiently sophisticated procurement staff with experience in defense systems; or when a purchasing government is seeking to establish a relationship between a U.S. manufacturer and its own domestic industry.

An extensive comparison of the advantages of FMS and DCS has been compiled and published by the Defense Institute of Security Assistance Management (DISAM) in Chapter 15 of its textbook, "The Management of Security Cooperation" - also referred to as "The Green Book".

The U.S. DoD is generally neutral as to whether a sale should be accomplished using the FMS or the DCS process. However, as a matter of policy, the USG will not entertain a potential FMS case with your country if you are already engaged in DCS discussions with a U.S. contractor.

There are times when the DoD requires that a purchase be accomplished through the FMS system. For example, the DoD requires all U.S. military training to be obtained through FMS. The DoD may also require defense articles to be sold "FMS-only." Two common reasons for this are to ensure the security of sensitive technologies and the control of weapons and munitions to prevent proliferation. There is no single list of all FMS-only items. Instead, the cognizant U.S. MILDEP (Army, Navy, Air Force), or the U.S. manufacturer, will tell you whether or not a particular item is FMS-only.

Hybrid Sales

It is possible to separate the FMS-only portions of a purchase from those portions permitted to be sold via DCS. And it is common for a foreign government to mix FMS and DCS when making major purchases of complex systems, such as aircraft. These are known as hybrid sales and might, for example, involve purchase of an airframe through DCS, and avionics, weapons, and training through FMS. If you are initiating a DCS purchase with a company and expect that it will (or might) include items that will be purchased via the FMS system, you should contact the appropriate U.S. MILDEP or DSCA as early as possible. The delivery timeline of your DCS end-item will likely depend in great measure upon FMS items being integrated first, or upon FMS training being provided at the appropriate time. It is therefore important that you discuss your larger purchase plans and your operational objectives with the appropriate MILDEP or DSCA to obtain an expert assessment and firm understanding of the FMS timeline and any potential issues. The defense contractor you are working with may not have full knowledge of Military Department plans and timelines. Therefore, the best source of information on any equipment that is to be provided by the USG is the USG itself.

Leases

Another method of obtaining defense articles from the U.S. is the use of a lease. The USG may lease defense articles to another country for temporary use (not to exceed five years). Leases can be entered into for a variety of purposes, including cooperative research or development, military exercises, and communications or electronics interface projects. Countries may also use a lease to fill a critical defense requirement while waiting for a delivery of items purchased through FMS or DCS. More detail on leases can be found in Section 11.6. of the SAMM.

Excess Defense Articles (EDA)

When defense articles are declared excess by the U.S. DoD, they may be transferred by sale (FMS) or by grant to countries eligible to receive EDA. Keep in mind however, that not all excess DoD articles are made available for sale or grant; and U.S. government agencies are given the first opportunity to acquire EDA items. For EDA sales to foreign customers, prices usually range from 5% to 50% of the original acquisition value, depending on the condition of the item. EDA is transferred on an "as-is, where-is" basis. This means that your country will be required to pay any repair and refurbishment costs, if necessary, and, generally, all transportation costs associated with getting the EDA items to your country. More detail on EDA can be found in Section 11.3. of the SAMM.

The above options may be used in different combinations to satisfy your country's unique requirements. A security cooperation program might consist of some items purchased through FMS, additional items through DCS, and still others obtained via lease. The USG can work with you to help you achieve the best "fit" for your needs.

Eligibility

The USG may sell, grant, or lease defense articles and services to a country or international organization only if the President makes a determination that the prospective purchaser is eligible based on criteria summarized in SAMM Section 4.1. SAMM Table C4.T2. contains a list of all countries, annotating those that are currently eligible or ineligible to participate in the U.S. FMS program.

For countries determined by the President to be eligible to participate in the U.S. FMS process, the Secretary of State determines whether the U.S. will support a given sale, grant, or lease to a country and the amount thereof. Because so many things are taken into consideration when determining whether or not the USG will support a given request for defense articles and services - see SAMM Section 4.2. - decisions are ultimately made on a case-by-case basis. Proposed sales that include technologically or politically sensitive elements can take more time - so, as a general principle, the sooner you make the USG aware of your interest in acquiring a capability or an item, the better.

Major USG Stakeholders in FMS

There are a great many USG organizations involved with various aspects of FMS. The below list is not all-inclusive, but does highlight some of the key players you should know about. See SAMM Section C1.3. for a more extensive description of USG responsibilities and relationships related to Security Assistance.

The United States Congress

By law, potential sales that meet certain criteria must be submitted for Congressional review over a specific time before these LOAs may be offered to foreign purchasers. The SAMM describes the Congressional Notification process in SAMM Section C5.5. We'll also discuss it further later in this guide.

The Department of State (DoS)

The Secretary of State is responsible for management and supervision of all aspects of U.S. security cooperation programs - including FMS. The DOS determines whether (and when) there will be a U.S. program with, or sale to, a particular country and, if so, its size and scope.

The DOS Bureau of Political Military Affairs office of Regional Security and Arms Transfers (PM/RSAT) is the lead DOS bureau for FMS matters, including transfer approvals and the notifications that must go to the U.S. Congress before a transfer can occur.

The DOS also reviews and approves export license requests for DCS of items on the United States Munitions List (USML), which is Part 121 of the International Traffic in Arms Regulations (ITAR). The DOS Directorate of Defense Trade Controls (DDTC) processes requests for commercial licenses for DCS. Defense articles and services sold through the FMS process do not require commercial export licenses - although a similar process of review is used.

The Department of Defense (DoD)

The Secretary of Defense establishes military requirements and implements programs to transfer defense articles and services to eligible foreign countries and international organizations. This is done in close coordination with the DOS.

The Under Secretary of Defense for Policy (USD(P)) serves as the principal staff assistant and advisor to the Secretary of Defense on security cooperation matters.

The Director of the Defense Security Cooperation Agency (DSCA) reports to the USD(P) and administers and supervises the execution of all security cooperation programs for the DoD. DSCA assigns Country Program Directors (CPDs) responsibility for all security cooperation activities for a country (or several countries). The CPD is always a good place to start with any questions you have - whether specifically about your country's program or about Security Cooperation in general. If you do not know who your CPD is, you can contact DSCA to find out. The CPD can also locate the appropriate policy and process experts within DSCA to help you through any of these security cooperation programs.

The Defense Technology Security Administration (DTSA) is the DoD Agency responsible for formulating DoD positions on proposed exports. DTSA provides those positions to the DOS as part of the DOS decision-making process when considering the approval or disapproval of a proposed sale of military equipment - whether FMS or DCS. When developing a position on the potential sale of a particular item to a foreign country, DTSA works in close coordination with experts in the Army, Navy, Air Force, and DSCA.

Military Departments (MILDEPs). In coordination with DSCA and the USD(P), the MILDEPs serve as advisors to the Secretary of Defense on all Security Cooperation matters related to their respective Departments (Army, Navy, and Air Force). They conduct military education and training and sales of defense articles and defense services to eligible foreign countries and international organizations in accordance with policies and criteria established by the Director, DSCA. They also provide technical information and data on weapons systems, tactics, doctrine, training, capabilities, logistic support, price, source, availability, and lead-time for a proposed FMS sale. Each MILDEP is primarily responsible for building and maintaining capability for U.S. military forces. As an added responsibility, the MILDEPs execute foreign sales and training as FMS "Implementing Agencies". For this, they each have organizations dedicated to FMS and to international training.

Department of the Army

The Deputy Assistant Secretary of the Army for Defense Exports and Cooperation (DASA [DE&C]), located in the Washington DC area, has Department of the Army policy oversight responsibility for international affairs functions, to include FMS.

The U.S. Army Security Assistance Command (USASAC), in Huntsville, Alabama, provides management oversight of all Army Security Cooperation programs.

The Army Security Assistance Training Field Activity (SATFA), at Fort Monroe, Virginia, is the U.S. Army's agent for Army international education and training. It supplies training support to foreign governments and serves as the focal point for all Army security cooperation training programs.

Department of the Navy

The Navy International Programs Office (IPO), in Washington, DC, is responsible for providing policy oversight of all Navy, Marine Corps and Coast Guard Security Cooperation programs. Navy IPO assists countries with determining requirements, helps in the drafting of LORs, and has responsibility for drafting LOAs in coordination with the various systems commands (Sea Systems, Air Systems, etc.).

The Naval Education and Training Security Assistance Field Activity (NETSAFA) is the Navy's agent for Navy international education and training. It coordinates and supplies training support to foreign governments and serves as the focal point for all Navy security cooperation training programs.

The Headquarters, U.S. Coast Guard, International Affairs Staff for Security Assistance and International Training (G-CI) coordinates Coast Guard security cooperation policy and directs the performance of Coast Guard security cooperation programs on behalf of the Commandant of the Coast Guard. Under agreement between the Coast Guard and the Navy, Navy IPO provides support to Coast Guard G-CI in the planning and execution of Security Cooperation, to include FMS.

Department of the Air Force

The Deputy Under Secretary of the Air Force for International Affairs (SAF/IA), in Washington, DC, is responsible for providing policy oversight of all Air Force Security Cooperation programs, to include FMS.

The Air Force Security Assistance Command (AFSAC), in Dayton, Ohio, has management oversight responsibility for all Air Force Security Cooperation programs.

The Air Force Security Assistance Training Squadron (AFSAT), under the Air Education and Training Command (AETC), is the U.S. Air Force agent for Air Force international education and training. It coordinates and supplies training support to foreign governments and serves as the focal point for all Air Force security cooperation training programs.

MILDEP Case Manager

Each MILDEP assigns a Case Manager to serve as the focal point for a given FMS case you may have with that particular MILDEP. You could have more than one Case Manager at a MILDEP if you have separate FMS cases involving different programs. For example, you might have one Navy Case Manager for a riverine boat purchase and another who manages a Navy aircraft case for your country.

MILDEP Country Program Director

The MILDEP will also have a Country Program Director responsible for overseeing that MILDEP's security cooperation relationship with your country. To continue the previous example, the Navy Country Program Director would be responsible for monitoring and facilitating the progress of both of your Navy FMS cases - riverine boats and aircraft.

There are also other, more specialized, Implementing Agencies such as the National Geospatial-Intelligence Agency (NGA), the Defense Logistics Agency (DLA), the Missile Defense Agency (MDA), and the National Security Agency (NSA). A complete list of Implementing Agencies, and their contact information, can be found in SAMM Table C5.T2.

Security Cooperation Organizations (SCOs)

SCOs are comprised of U.S. military and civilian personnel the DoD stations overseas to manage security cooperation programs, to include security cooperation. The DoD has SCO personnel working in most of the U.S. embassies around the world. SCOs can place at your disposal the wealth of knowledge they possess within their organization, or they can contact subject matter experts in specialty areas to respond to detailed or technical questions you may have. You can contact the SCO through the Defense Attaché Office at the U.S. Embassy in your country. A list of all U.S. embassies and links to their websites can be found at http://www.usembassy.gov.

Other DoD organizations that play an important role in FMS include:

- The Defense Contract Management Agency (DCMA) which performs contract administration and management, quality assurance and inspection for the DoD, including contracts that support FMS cases;

- The <u>Defense Contract Audit Agency (DCAA)</u> which performs all necessary contract auditing for the both DoD purchases and FMS cases;

- The <u>Defense Finance and Accounting Service (DFAS)</u> which is responsible for accounting, billing, disbursing and collecting functions for the FMS program.

FMS - What Happens First

Defining Your Country's Requirements

Your government determines its security objectives based on its own unique situation and priorities. This typically involves conducting an assessment of your strategic and operational needs and capabilities, and then identifying specific items or training your country must acquire to close or narrow the gap between your defense needs and your existing capabilities.

If you would like the U.S. to assist in the conduct of an assessment - or any part of an assessment - you can contact the SCO in your country, the appropriate MILDEP Country Manager, or the DSCA Country Program Director. Any one of them can arrange for you to meet with U.S. experts to discuss requirements, constraints, timelines, and potential options. If needed, we can also arrange more extensive and specialized assistance such as survey teams. These activities can help inform the request your government ultimately submits to the USG. They can save you considerable time; they help ensure your staff and leadership fully understand all of the technical and programmatic issues involved with the proposed acquisition; and they make sure your country gets the best solution (weapons, services, training, construction, etc.) to match your operational requirement and budget. If your country requires extensive assistance, the USG may request that you open an FMS case to cover the cost.

The Letter of Request (LOR)

Although we recommend opening a dialogue with the U.S. DoD as soon as you identify a need for a particular capability, the action that formally begins the FMS process is your LOR.

If you are sending the LOR from your home country and have questions about how to prepare it, your first contact should be with the SCO for your country. SCO personnel understand the FMS process and can be a valuable source of information and advice. If you do not know whether you have a SCO in your country, you can easily find out by contacting the <u>U.S. Embassy</u>.

You may also refer questions to your DSCA Country Program Director or to the appropriate Implementing Agency, especially if you work from your embassy in Washington D.C., or from a liaison office located in the United States.

There is no set format for an LOR. It can be a formal letter, an e-mail, or even a verbal request from a recognized official representative of your government. There are three general types of LORs:

1. **LOR for Price and Availability (P&A).** These LORs are used by foreign customers to obtain basic information for further planning. In the LOR for P&A, you describe your requirement in as much detail as you have, and the USG replies with a rough estimate of the cost of the items and/or services you are interested in and an estimate of how long it would take the USG to deliver the item and/or service. It normally takes a MILDEP or other Implementing Agency about 45 days to respond to an LOR for P&A. It is important to keep in mind that P&A responses are Rough Order of Magnitude (ROM) estimates only. They do not constitute a commitment by the USG, and the data is used only for estimating P&A. If you decide to move to the next step and request an official government-to-government agreement, the MILDEP or other Implementing Agency will conduct a much more refined analysis resulting in a more accurate estimate for that agreement.

2. **LOR for a government-to-government Letter of Offer and Acceptance (LOA).** The submission of this type of LOR is viewed by the USG as an official expression of interest by your country, prompting the appropriate MILDEP or other Implementing Agency to develop the government-to-government LOA detailing the defense equipment and/or services the USG will provide and a "best-estimate" cost to you, the customer. Very often, a country will submit an LOR for P&A, and then, once the general cost and delivery schedule is understood, follow with an LOR for LOA.

3. **LOR for a change to an already existing LOA.** LORs are also used when you wish to request an Amendment or Modification to an existing LOA for which an FMS case has already been implemented. We will discuss Amendments and Modifications in more detail later in this guide.

LOR Guidance

Although there is no set format for an LOR, it needs to provide sufficient detail to allow a prompt and accurate response from the USG. SAMM Section C5.1.2. lists the minimum information that needs to be included in an LOR and SAMM Table C5.T3. describes the evaluation criteria the USG uses when determining whether or not a LOR contains all of the needed information. Appendix 1 of this guide provides additional information your government should consider when drafting an LOR.

While formal action must wait for receipt of a LOR, we encourage you to discuss complex LORs with the intended Implementing Agency prior to actually submitting the LOR to the USG. The Implementing Agency can assist you in developing or clarifying requirements. This helps ensure the LOR will request the equipment and services that will best meet your needs. Even if your country is very familiar with the FMS system, and has a clear understanding of your own equipment or training requirements, it would still be beneficial to contact the appropriate Implementing Agency prior to submitting your LOR since there could be any number of events on the U.S. side that might impact your FMS purchase, such as projected U.S. lot buys of the same item, planned upgrades, changes in contractors or subcontractors, or upcoming production line closures.

Requests that originate from within your country must be transmitted to the U.S. either by an authorized representative of your government or by the U.S. military representative at the U.S. Embassy in your country. LORs should be sent to the appropriate U.S. Implementing Agency and the Defense Security Cooperation Agency (DSCA) Operations Directorate. A list of all Implementing Agencies that process LORs, to include mailing addresses, is in SAMM Table C5.T2.

A more detailed guide to preparing LORs is available at Appendix 1 of this guide.

What Will We Do With Your LOR?

Each LOR is reviewed and validated by the MILDEP or other Implementing Agency and by DSCA to ensure that the prospective FMS purchaser is eligible, that the defense articles/services may be sold, that the request originated from a recognized official representative of your government, and that the LOR is clear and complete.

The Implementing Agency is responsible for taking action on your LOR. Based on your request the Implementing Agency will normally prepare one of the following:

- A Price and Availability (P&A) response
- A government-to-government Letter of Offer and Acceptance (LOA)
- An amendment to an LOA (if you've requested a change or addition to an existing LOA)
- A lease

For the purposes of this guide, we will assume that a new LOA is the most appropriate response to your request---therefore, the following USG actions would be taken:

- **We will acknowledge receipt:** Within five days of receipt of a valid LOR, the U.S. Implementing Agency will acknowledge receipt.
- **We may request more information:** If information is unclear or is missing from your LOR, the Implementing Agency will contact you to obtain the missing information so that the LOR will be "complete", meaning it contains enough information for the Implementing Agency to provide a response. While it may be possible to continue limited processing of some portions of the request, a response from the USG may be delayed until the information is provided or the request amended.
- **We will assign an FMS case identifier:** An FMS case identifier is assigned to each LOR. A case identifier consists of a Country Code, the code of the Implementing Agency developing your FMS case, and a unique three-position FMS case designator. For example, "BN-B-UXP" is an FMS case for Bandaria ("BN"-an imaginary country) being prepared by the U.S. Army ("B" is the Implementing Agency code for the U.S. Army). The "UXP" is a unique code assigned to your FMS case for the defense item, service, or training you have requested.
- **We will assign an FMS Case Manager:** An FMS Case Manager is assigned to every FMS case and is responsible for ensuring that the FMS case meets your requirements as identified in your LOR. The FMS Case Manager acts as the coordinator for both development of the FMS case and the subsequent "execution," or performance of the FMS case. If you have questions about the progress of your FMS case, they should be directed to the appropriate FMS Case Manager. DSCA has assigned a Country Program Director (CPD) for each country and the Implementing Agency may also assign a Country Program Director for your programs. You may also contact these Program Directors if you have questions concerning the progress of your FMS case.
- **We will review the request to determine if there are any releasability issues:** Part of the USG review process involves determining if the technology involved is releasable for export. The releasability review takes place for both government-to-government FMS and for DCS that are directly negotiated between your country and a specific U.S. manufacturer. If the sale involves a system with technology that has not been previously approved for export to your country, this process will generally take longer than if the system has previously been reviewed and approved for export to your country. The DoD reviews each proposed sale or transfer of

defense items or services and then provides a recommendation to the DOS. But only the DOS - not the DoD - has authority under U.S. law to approve the sale or transfer to a foreign country. Because there can be so many variables involved, it is often difficult to estimate with accuracy the amount of time a technology release review will take but, generally speaking, if sensitive technologies are involved, the sooner you can begin a dialogue with the Implementing Agency, the better.

- **We will notify the U.S. Congress, if necessary:** If a potential sale exceeds certain dollar thresholds, U.S. law requires that the sale be approved by the U.S. Congress prior to the USG offering an LOA to the requesting country. A complete list of Congressional Notification requirements can be found at SAMM Section C5.T13. In general, the thresholds are:

	NATO (+5)*	All Other Countries
Major Defense Equipment (MDE)	$25 million	$14 million
Articles/Services	$100 million	$50 million
Construction	$300 million	$200 million
* "+5" = Australia, Israel, Japan, South Korea & New Zealand		

MDE means any item in the International Traffic in Arms Regulation (ITAR) on the U.S. Munitions List (USML) that:

a) Warrants special export controls (we call these items Significant Military Equipment (SME)) and mark them with an asterisk in the USML; and
b) That have a nonrecurring Research and Development cost of $50 million or more or a total production cost of $200 million or more.

A list of MDE is contained in Appendix 1 of the SAMM. This notification process must be completed before the LOA can be formally offered to your country for consideration. When the official notification of a sale has been made to the U.S. Congress, this information is posted to the "Major Arms Sales" page of the DSCA Web Site.

The formal Congressional Notification period is 30 days (15 days for NATO (+5)), meaning that if no Congressional objection is raised prior to expiration of the 30-day period the sale may go forward. This does not include the 10-20 days the Implementing Agency and DSCA take to prepare the notification and coordinate it with the DOS. Lastly, in order for formal notification to occur, Congress (both the House and the Senate) must be in session for at least one day during the formal notification period. The SAMM provides a more thorough discussion of Congressional notification requirements and process at SAMM Section C5.5.

The Letter of Offer and Acceptance (LOA)

As mentioned earlier, the LOA is the government-to-government agreement that identifies the defense articles and services the USG proposes to sell to your country to meet the requirements identified in your LOR.

The Implementing Agency with responsibility for the item requested by your country will prepare the LOA. There are three basic types of FMS cases. The type used depends on what is being sold:

1. **Defined Order:** This type of FMS case is for defense articles and/or services that are specified in your LOR and stated explicitly in the LOA. A Defined Order FMS case would most likely be used for purchasing major end items, such as trucks, and for weapon system sales. When discussing Defined Order FMS cases, the USG will further distinguish between those that are relatively simple to execute because they are for standard items, such as 5-ton trucks, and those that are complex and involve purchaser-unique considerations, such as fighter aircraft.

2. **Blanket Order:** Used to purchase a specific category of items or services at a set dollar value ceiling with no definitive listing of the exact items or quantities desired. This type would most likely be used for follow-on support items such as spare and repair parts. Normally a blanket order case is used for follow-on support and training for a major item or weapon system following the initial support period of a Defined Order FMS case. A Blanket Order case remains open as long as it has funds against it. The case can be extended simply by requesting an Amendment to add funding.

3. **Cooperative Logistics Supply Support Arrangement (CLSSA):** Permits your country to participate in the U.S. supply system so that you can draw frequently used parts and other supplies from U.S. stocks based on demand rates the way that U.S. military units do. Each CLSSA consists of two separate FMS cases, one for the U.S. to purchase and sustain the spare and repair parts, and one that the FMS customer uses to order parts and replenish the stocks. CLSSA increases the probability of spare parts being available for issue from U.S. stock.

You can find more information on the types of FMS cases at SAMM Section C5.4.3.

Two FMS Information Technology Systems You Should Know About

1. **The Defense Security Assistance Management System (DSAMS).** DSAMS is a DoD standard system used to develop and track the progress of FMS cases. It contains detailed information on FMS case development and implementation. DSAMS contains information on every FMS case and on any amendments or modifications to each case. The Implementing Agency inputs case information into DSAMS and DSAMS produces LOAs for USG and partner nation approval and signature. DSAMS tracks the progress of an FMS case's life - from development to execution, to closure - through the use of milestones. DSAMS is for U.S. government use only, but it feeds information to another information technology system - the Security Cooperation Information Portal - that provides access to FMS customers.

2. **The Security Cooperation Information Portal (SCIP).** SCIP provides visibility of your country's FMS case(s) to authorized users, anywhere in the world, using any common web browser. SCIP data is automatically drawn from DSAMS, MILDEP computer systems, and other financial and logistic systems and consolidated for use within SCIP. You can even track delivery through an Enhanced Freight Tracking System (EFTS) feature. SCIP can produce either standard automated reports or unique reports you design yourself. DSCA limits access to SCIP to designated USG employees and to representatives of FMS purchaser countries. U.S. access is controlled through our government Common Access Card (CAC). Non-USG access is controlled through electronic USB "tokens" we distribute to non-USG SCIP users. We further limit access such that USG employees can view information related only to countries for which they are responsible, and foreign representatives can view information related only to their own country.
If you would like instructions for establishing a SCIP account, see Appendix 1: How to establish a SCIP account. From within SCIP, you can access information on an FMS case from the time an LOR is first received and logged into the MILDEP computer system and track it through the case development and execution process.

LOA Preparation Time

The time required to prepare LOAs varies with the complexity of the sale and the clarity of the information provided in the LOR. Processing time for LOAs and Amendments is measured from the time the LOR is received at the Implementing Agency until the time the LOA is offered to you, the purchaser. When the Implementing Agency receives your country's LOR, it establishes an Anticipated Offer Date (AOD) and enters it into DSAMS, which then feeds the information into SCIP, where you can view it. The Implementing Agency must develop the LOA and provide it to your country for signature by the AOD. The AOD standard by which Implementing Agencies are held is:

- 30 days for Blanket Order LOAs, CLSSAs, and training LOAs.
- 30 days for Defined Order LOAs.
- 90 days for Defined Order LOAs and associated Amendments that are considered "purchaser-unique". The Implementing Agency may determine an FMS case will be "purchaser-unique" if it meets one or more of the following criteria:
  - A first-time purchase of a defense article or service by an FMS purchaser
  - A first-time FMS purchase by a specific country or international organization with limited experience or knowledge of FMS processes/procedures
  - The case requires engineering, system integration, or special acquisition
  - The requested use of the system is different from its use by U.S. military forces (e.g., Navy ship missile to be fired from an Army or foreign country helicopter)
  - Detailed release/disclosure coordination is required
  - Complex pricing effort is required
  - Extraordinary coordination required inside or outside the Implementing Agency
  - Other (requires an explanation be entered into DSAMS)

Thus, the maximum processing time between an Implementing Agency's receipt of your LOR and release of the LOA or Amendment for your country's signature should normally be no more than 90 days if the proposed sale does not require significant technology release and is below Congressional notification thresholds.

An Implementing Agency must move quickly to provide you with an LOA within the time limits allowed. It must solicit any remaining information needed from your country, build a program that meets your operational, budgetary and timeline requirements and, often in coordination with commercial vendors, develop cost estimates for every item that makes up your overall program. This is why, at least for more complex purchases, it may be helpful for you to contact the Implementing Agency to discuss your potential purchase in detail before you submit your LOR.

What Happens After Your LOA is Prepared?

Once the FMS case has been written, it is reviewed by the originating Implementing Agency's staff and DSCA staff to ensure it meets the requirements of your LOR and U.S. laws and regulations. After it has been approved by the Implementing Agency and DSCA, the LOA is submitted to the DOS for review and approval. It is then countersigned by DSCA, signed by the Implementing Agency, and transmitted to your country for review and signature by your approving authority.

What Will the LOA Look Like?

Much of the content of an LOA, especially the Standard Terms and Conditions, is dictated by U.S. law. A great deal of useful information about LOAs can be found in Chapter 5 of the SAMM. In particular:

- <u>Figure C5.F3.</u> contains a sample LOA
- <u>Figure C5.F4.</u> provides all of the Standard Terms and Conditions that accompany any LOA
- <u>Figure C5.F5.</u> explains all of the information and codes contained in an LOA

LOA Sections

Your LOA will be made up of several sections. The first page will be an overview of the proposal and will include a space for the signatures of our USG representative and your government's representative. It will provide a total cost estimate and will identify any initial deposit that might be required upon acceptance. The first page will also include the expiration date of the USG offer - or Offer Expiration Date (OED).

The next several pages of the LOA will describe in greater detail the material and services being offered and responsibilities for transportation and delivery of the items. Separate FMS "case lines" will be included on your LOA. Each line will cover a specific category of material or service. Most of the information is in plain text or monetary terms, but in several situations we use codes to convey information. The codes are explained in detail in the "<u>Letter of Offer and Acceptance Information</u>" provided with each FMS case.

A sample FMS case line might look like the following:

(1)	(2)	(3)	(4)		(5)	(6)	(7)
Itm Nbr	Description / Condition	Qty, Unit of Issue	(a) Unit	(b) Total	SC/MOS/TA	Ofr Rel Cde	Del Trm Cde
001	E3Z 23200014120143 (N) HMMWV M1113 Truck, Shelter Carrier with Desert Package, including CTIS, Sand Colored Paint (CARC 686)	20 EA	$71,333.52	$1,426,671	P(18) TA5 NR	Y	4

The LOA will include a cost summary and an estimated payment schedule along with instructions on where to return the signed LOA and how to submit payments.

The LOA will include special notes - commonly referred to as "case notes" - to provide additional information unique to the FMS case.

The case notes will be followed by "<u>Standard Terms and Conditions</u>" - commonly referred to as "standard notes". These are included with every FMS case we write. They are not unique to your particular country or FMS case.

LOA Pricing and Delivery Estimates

Dollar values and delivery schedules shown on the LOA are estimates based on the best available information at the time the LOA is prepared. During the life of the FMS case, the amounts billed to the FMS case will be the actual costs incurred by the USG. This may differ from the estimate included in the LOA.

- **Administrative Surcharge.** DSCA adds a 3.5% fee to all FMS sales to cover costs associated with administering the FMS program, including facilities, information systems, and civilian employee salaries.
- **Contract Administration Services (CAS).** The USG charges a separate 1.5% fee to cover quality assurance and inspection, contract audits, and related services conducted primarily by the U.S. DoD acquisition and logistics community.

- **Non-Recurring Research and Development (R&D) Costs.** Your country may be charged a fee to pay a pro-rata share of the non-recurring research and development costs incurred by the U.S. government in the development of the weapon system being purchased.
- **Other Potential Fees.** All potential fees are discussed in SAMM Section C9.5. Waivers to fees are covered in SAMM Section C9.6.

Payment Schedule

The LOA will include an estimated payment schedule identifying when each of your payments is due. The schedule consists of two financial categories: (1) your initial deposit, and (2) future estimated quarterly billing amounts. Your initial deposit is for the costs anticipated to be incurred from FMS case acceptance until your first quarterly FMS billing statement is provided and monies collected. If the FMS case is written as "cash with acceptance," the initial deposit will be for the entire FMS case value. Some of the factors used in computing your payment schedule include:

- **Progress Payments:** Those payments made to contractors or DoD activities as work progresses under a contract.
- **Contractor Holdback:** Amount earned by contractors or suppliers during the period but held back by the USG to ensure future performance of the contractor.
- **Termination Liability:** That amount collected from you in advance to protect the USG if you decide to terminate a program before performance is complete.

Note: If your country has any unique payment schedule requirements due to its budget cycle or budget development process, you should discuss them with the Implementing Agency as early as possible and/or include those requirements in the LOR.

Your Review and Response to an LOA

LOA Acceptance

An Offer Expiration Date (OED) will be identified on the LOA. Normally you will have sixty (60) days to review and sign the LOA. If you know that the OED cannot be met, you should request an extension from the Implementing Agency as soon as possible. Extensions may be granted as long as the pricing and delivery estimates are expected to remain valid for the extended time period.

Of course, part of your review will be to determine if the proposed items and costs meet your country's needs and budgetary constraints. If you want to request any changes to the offer based on your review, your change request must be submitted to the Implementing Agency for consideration prior to your acceptance (signature) of the LOA. Simple "pen and ink" changes to an LOA may be accepted by the Implementing Agency prior to FMS case signature if the changes are relatively minor administrative or corrective changes. If the "pen and ink" change would alter the scope or revise the terms of sale or the total costs, this would normally be considered a "counter offer" - essentially a new LOR. Similarly, if your government signs an LOA that includes changes that have not been agreed-to by the Implementing Agency in advance, we will consider it to be a counter-offer. Depending upon the extent of the proposed changes, the LOA may be re-stated and re-offered, or a new LOA might be prepared.

The name, title, and agency of the signing official must be entered as well as the date of acceptance/signature (on or before the OED).

The initial deposit is an integral part of acceptance and is also required on or before the OED. The LOA contains instructions for sending the required initial payment to the Defense Finance and Accounting Service (DFAS). Payment must be in U.S. dollars and may be transmitted by check or wire transfer.

After Acceptance

FMS Case Implementation and Execution

Once the USG has received a signed copy of the LOA and the initial deposit, the FMS case will be implemented so that execution (contract negotiations, requisitioning, etc.) may begin.

On receipt of the initial deposit, the Defense Finance and Accounting Office (DFAS) grants the Implementing Agency authority to begin obligating funds to execute your country's FMS case. The Implementing Agency can then begin procurement of the defense articles and/or services.

A major FMS case will typically include items from U.S. government stocks as well as procurement of items from new production. Items to be procured are contracted from defense industry by the appropriate U.S. government procurement offices. For example, the Air Force Program Office responsible for overseeing procurement of C-17 cargo aircraft for the U.S. Air Force will also be responsible for procuring C-17 cargo aircraft for an FMS case.

Changes During the Life of Your FMS Program

Occasionally, during the life of your FMS program, changes will need to be made to the LOA. An error may need to be corrected, your country may want to add additional items or quantities, or you may want to add or reduce the value of the FMS case. Depending upon what needs to be done and why, the changes may be initiated by the USG or by you. These changes will take the form of Amendments or Modifications.

Amendments: Any revision to an LOA that requires your acceptance must be done using an Amendment. Amendments might include changes in the scope of an FMS case, such as the type or number of items to be provided. Before they can be implemented, Amendments must be accepted by both the USG and by you, the FMS customer, in the same manner as the original LOA. Some Amendments may require initial deposits - just like basic cases; these funds must be received before the Amendment will be implemented. As with Basic LOAs, "pen and ink" changes can be made to LOA Amendments. To learn more about LOA Amendments and when it is appropriate to use them, see SAMM Section C6.7.1.

Modifications: Any revision that does not require your government's acceptance may be done using a Modification. Modifications do not change the scope of a case (such as the type or number of items being purchased) and are usually used to correct administrative errors or for unilateral USG changes that must be made to the case. Remember, the information in an LOA constitutes the USG's best estimate of what an item or service will cost and when it can be delivered. If that estimate changes (due, for instance, to a shortage of a particular item causing a slowdown in overall production), the USG may need to adjust the LOA accordingly. Although customer acceptance of a Modification is not necessary, the Implementing Agency will provide a copy to your country's authorized representative for the FMS case and request acknowledgement. Except for DSCA-issued changes to an LOA's financing terms, pen and ink changes to Modifications are not authorized. Changes initiated after a Modification has been implemented must be accomplished using another Modification or Amendment, as appropriate. To learn more about LOA Modifications and when it is appropriate to use them, see SAMM Section C6.7.2.

Cancellations: It is possible for your country to cancel an FMS case after it has been implemented. However, because the USG can neither profit from nor lose money in the execution of an FMS case on behalf of a foreign country, your government will be responsible for any termination costs (any up-front costs the contractor has already incurred in producing, or preparing to produce the defense articles ordered on the FMS case) as well as any USG administrative costs associated with the case. The SAMM discusses Cancellations in Section C6.8.

Case Closure: Case Closure can begin when all conditions of the LOA are satisfied - meaning, among other things, that all supplies and services have been delivered to your government and all warranty periods have elapsed. We call this "Supply and Services Complete". See SAMM Section C16.2.12. for more detail about what constitutes supply and services complete. Aside from bringing an FMS case to successful conclusion, case closure is often important to an FMS customer because it permits the return of any surplus funds to that government for use toward other projects. Key to closure is the reconciliation of financial information with supply and logistics status - essentially, it amounts to confirming that your country received what it was supposed to, at the correct cost, and that the USG will not be left with any debts or extra funds. U.S. law forbids either. For more complex cases, the reconciliation and case closure process can sometimes be lengthy. Reconciliation for closure begins at Supply and Services Complete and continues until the case is "final" closed. However, active case review and reconciliation should occur throughout the life of every FMS case, from LOA implementation until the case is Supply and Services Complete. The Implementing Agency Case Manager is responsible for reconciliation. The quality of the active reconciliation that occurs from LOA implementation to Supply and Service Complete will directly impact the speed and level of difficulty of the closure reconciliation. Chapter 16 of the SAMM is dedicated to Case Closure and Reconciliation.

After Delivery

End Use Monitoring (EUM)

According to U.S. law, before the DoD may transfer defense articles, training, and services to another country, the recipient governments must agree to use U.S.-provided defense articles, training, and services only for their intended purpose; not to transfer title to, or possession of, any defense article or related training to anyone not an officer, employee, or agent of that country or of the USG without prior written consent of the USG; to maintain the security of any article with substantially the same degree of protection afforded to it by the USG; and to permit observation and review by, and to furnish necessary information to, representatives of the USG with regards to use of such articles. These obligations are stipulated in the Standard Terms and Conditions of every LOA. End Use Monitoring helps the DoD verify the obligations are being met.

Post-delivery monitoring is normally performed by USG personnel - usually military - assigned to the Security Cooperation Office (SCO) in your country. SCOs employ two post-delivery monitoring methodologies to perform the U.S. Department of Defense's EUM responsibilities: Routine End Use Monitoring and Enhanced End Use Monitoring. In both instances, the SCO coordinates with your government to schedule EUM.

Routine EUM is required for all defense articles and services provided via government-to-government programs. SCO personnel perform Routine EUM in conjunction with other security cooperation functions, during visits to the host nation's installations, through interaction with other assigned embassy personnel, and from any other readily available or opportune source of information.

Enhanced EUM is required for defense articles and services or for individual transfers specifically designated for Enhanced Monitoring. All EEUM-designated defense articles are accompanied by specialized physical security and accountability notes in the LOA. Defense articles listed in SAMM Table C8.T4. are designated for EEUM for all FMS-eligible countries. Other defense articles may require EEUM on a case-by-case basis as a result of the transfer approval process.

More information on Routine and Enhanced EUM can be found at SAMM Chapter 8.

Third-Party Transfers or Change in End-Use

During the above discussion of End Use Monitoring, we noted that the LOA Standard Terms and Conditions require governments receiving U.S. defense articles and services to agree not to transfer title or possession of those articles or services to anyone not an officer, employee, or agent of that country or of the USG without prior written consent from the USG. Also, the recipient country must agree not to use or permit the use of the articles or services for purposes other than for which they were furnished unless the foreign government receives prior written consent from the USG. Please note:

- The LOA stipulations apply to all equipment transferred on an LOA, no matter its age or condition. For instance, an old or damaged airplane or armored personnel carrier could not be turned over to a private company as scrap or placed in a government museum as a display - until the USG agreed in writing to the third-party transfer in the first instance; or to the change in end-use in the second instance.
- The agreement also applies to training. For example, if the U.S. provides your Air Force with aircraft maintenance training, that knowledge could not later be shared with another country without prior written USG consent.
- The Department of State Office of Regional Security and Arms Transfer Policy (PM/RSAT) is responsible for authorizing third party transfers of U.S.-origin defense articles and/or services worldwide. The PM/RSAT website contains detailed information about the third party transfer process and documentation. The SAMM discusses third party transfer and changes in end-use in SAMM Section 8.7.

Learn More about Security Assistance

The Security Assistance Management Manual (SAMM)

The SAMM is the authoritative document on Security Cooperation policy and procedures. In April 2012, the SAMM was converted into a fully-digital electronic version (E-SAMM) that can be found at http://www.samm.dsca.mil.

At the site, visitors can view the SAMM and all policy memorandums released by DSCA. The E-SAMM has a very good search function to help you find information in the SAMM or in DSCA Policy Memos. Once at the Search page, click on the "Advanced Search" button to select areas of the SAMM and/or Policy Memos you would like to search. Once at an E-SAMM chapter, you can search that chapter for a given word or phrase by clicking on "edit" within Microsoft Internet Explorer and then clicking "find on this page".

The Defense Institute for Security Assistance Management (DISAM)

DISAM teaches all aspects of FMS and Security Cooperation to military, government, industry, and foreign representatives. The DISAM webpage is at http://www.disam.dsca.mil. DISAM has an extensive list of course offerings for foreign students in its catalogue. DISAM also makes available a number of useful publications, including the textbook it uses for instruction. The text is revised annually and is commonly referred to as the "Green Book" as it is bound in a green cover. The Green Book and other DISAM publications, including many designed specifically for foreign customers, can be viewed and downloaded at DISAM's publications site. DISAM also posts informative presentations to their website so that anyone can view and download them. Finally, the DISAM web site has an "Ask an Instructor" feature that allows anyone to pose questions to their faculty.

The Defense Security Cooperation Agency (DSCA)

DSCA staff can provide you with a wealth of information. The starting point should the DSCA Country Program Director (CPD) responsible for working with your country. If you do not know who this is or do not have your CPD's contact information, you can contact the DSCA headquarters and we will connect you with your country's CPD.

The appropriate Implementing Agency (IA)

If you have questions that relate to a specific MILDEP (Army, Navy, or Air Force) or to some other Implementing Agency, you can contact that organization directly. A list of Implementing Agencies and their contact information can be found in SAMM Table C5.T2. If you have trouble, feel free to contact your DSCA CPD for assistance.

The Security Cooperation Organization (SCO) in your country

If it is more convenient to talk with someone within your own country, you can contact the SCO personnel stationed at the U.S. Embassy in your capital city. A list of all U.S. embassies and links to their websites is located at http://www.usembassy.gov/. You can reach the SCO through the Defense Attaché Office, which should have contact information listed under the embassy's "Sections and Offices" link in the drop-down menu that appears after clicking on the "about us" tab of any official U.S. Embassy web site.

Appendix 1 - Letter of Request (LOR) Guide

The action that formally begins the FMS process is the Letter of Request, or "LOR". The LOR is a document generated by a purchasing government and submitted to the USG. It can be either a request for the purchase of defense articles or services, or it can request rough-estimate Price and Availability (P&A) data to help your government decide whether or not to pursue a purchase further. LOR's can be submitted through formal correspondence, as a request for proposal (RFP's), or via discussions, e-mail, letters, or messages. In replying to an LOR, the Implementing Agency will prepare either an LOA for an FMS case, or P&A data, whichever you requested.

Format

There is no set format for an LOR. It can be provided to the USG in most any format so long as we know it has been transmitted by an official representative of your government and it contains at least the minimum required information.

Submission

SAMM Section C5.1.3. describes the LOR channels of submission procedures. DSCA and the applicable Implementing Agency should be action addressees on all LORs, with copies provided to the SCO and the Regional Combatant Command (CENTCOM, PACOM, SOUTHCOM, EUCOM, AFRICOM, or NORTHCOM). Requests for Significant Military Equipment (SME) and Major Defense Equipment (MDE) should also be provided to the Department of State Political-Military Affairs (PM) Bureau. See SAMM Section C5.1.3. for additional information on SME and MDE requests. If you are not sure whether the items you are requesting are SME, MDE, or neither, you can ask the U.S. Security Cooperation Organization at the U.S. embassy in your country, the MILDEP/Implementing Agency, or DSCA for assistance.

Minimum Information Requirements

There are many things that should be considered and included when developing an LOR to purchase a defense article or service from the DoD. The detail of the LOR will depend upon the type of case - whether blanket, CLSSA, or defined - and the sophistication of the weapon system requested.

SAMM Section C5.1.2. lists seven LOR information requirements. They are:

1. Identify the desired defense articles and/or services in sufficient detail for the United States Government (USG) to prepare an accurate cost estimate;
2. Indicate whether Price and Availability (P&A) data, a Letter of Offer and Acceptance (LOA), or an LOA Amendment or LOA Modification is desired;
3. If for a blanket order LOA (SAMM Section C5.4.3.2.) or CLSSA (SAMM Section C5.4.3.3.), include the desired materiel and services value or the desired total case value;
4. Indicate the proposed method of financing (your own national funds, U.S. Foreign Military Financing (FMF), etc.)
5. Identify any anticipated involvement in the requested case by anyone not a duly appointed officer or government civilian employee of the requesting government - i.e., a "third party" - so that the receiving Military Department (MILDEP)/Implementing Agency (IA) may initiate appropriate reviews and approval requests;
6. Contain the name and address of the originator and a traceable reference number, such as a letter serial number; and

7. Identify the intended/anticipated recipient unit for any defense articles and/or services to be purchased with Foreign Military Financing (FMF) funds, recognizing such unit designations may change as the case is implemented and equipment is delivered to the host nation. The SCO will update the recipient unit designation at the time of LOA signature, if applicable, by alerting the IA who will input updated information into DSAMS.

Some LORs, such as Blanket Order or CLSSA cases or follow-on LORs to change already-existing LOAs, are often very simple, and so completing the first information requirement and providing "sufficient detail" is relatively quick and easy. LOAs for these FMS cases reflect categories of items (normally to support one or more end items) with no itemized list or quantities. For instance, your LOR may be for a Blanket Order FMS case or CLSSA to support C-130 and F-16 spare parts with a total FMS case value of $1,000,000; or it might simply request a "Blanket Order FMS case for training".

Defined Order cases range from relatively uncomplicated - such as buying standard end-items like cargo trucks, to very complex - such as major aircraft purchases. In the former instance, an FMS customer would need to specify the number and type of trucks and the desired configuration, and then might need to provide some additional detail on things like paint type and color scheme, spare and repair parts, tool sets, diagnostic and calibration equipment, extreme cold weather kits, and driver and maintenance training. For the more complex requests, the USG will need significantly more information to respond quickly with an offer that fully meets your country's needs.

Complex FMS Purchases

An Implementing Agency is limited in what it can do with a less-than-complete LOR. So, for more complex purchases, you should include as much detail as possible in the LOR. If at all possible, consult with the appropriate Implementing Agency before submitting the LOR so that it contains all of the necessary information when submitted. Some MILDEPS have useful tools you can use when drafting your LOR:

- **Army:** The U.S. Army Security Assistance Command (USASAC) posts LOR checklists for many of its most commonly requested systems at the International Customers tab at the USASAC Website.
- **Air Force:** The U.S. Air Force Security Assistance Center (AFSAC) also posts LOR checklists for its commonly requested systems at the "Letter of Request Preparation" tab under "Application Links" in the toolbar on the left-hand side of the AFSAC webpage. On the same webpage, you can request access to AFSAC's Automated LOR tool. Click on the "Letter of Request Submission" tab under "Application Links" in the toolbar on the left side of the AFSAC Webpage and then click on "LOR Automated Tool". To use the Automated LOR tool, you must have (or establish) a user account. To establish a new user account for the U.S. Air Force Automated LOR tool, follow the instructions listed on the site.
- **Navy:** The U.S. Navy International Programs Office (Navy IPO) is in the process of adopting an Automated LOR tool. Until such time as the Navy Automated LOR tool is active, you can contact the Navy IPO or the appropriate Navy Systems Command (e.g. Navy Sea Systems (NAVSEA) Command, or Navy Air Systems (NAVAIR) Command) to discuss the LOR you are drafting.

In instances in which your country submits an LOR but is not familiar enough with the particular U.S. weapon system to be able to include adequate detail, the Implementing Agency will contact you to begin discussing the details needed to make the LOR "complete" - i.e. something the Implementing Agency can use to offer you a well thought-out program. These discussions might be accomplished via e-mail or telephone - or they may require face-to-face meetings at which the Implementing Agency provides you and your subject matter experts with enough information about the weapon system, and the training and support requirements that come with it, so that your government can clarify its needs.

In some instances, to fully understand your country's requirements and to ensure the weapon system's configuration and support package are properly matched to your situation, the Implementing Agency may need to do more detailed assessments and/or site surveys. If this sort of extensive technical assistance is needed, the USG may request that your country submit a LOR for a technical assistance case to fund the additional work.

The dialogue between you and the Implementing Agency will ensure your country gets the most accurate LOA possible and, ultimately, the right equipment for your country's needs. However, you should understand that, if only initiated after LOR submission, it could increase the time between when your country's LOR was submitted and the USG response in the form of an LOA. The Implementing Agency can proceed with incomplete information if necessary, but doing so increases the risk the LOA will not adequately reflect your country's needs and have to be re-done (we call it "restating the LOA").

Building the LOR - General Guidance

When developing an LOA response to your country's LOR, the USG takes a "systems" approach - generally referred to as the "Total Package Approach" (See SAMM Section C4.3.2.). U.S. experts, with years of experience behind them, design a program that takes everything into consideration - your operational requirements, your affordability targets, your delivery schedule, and all of the related logistics, maintenance, transportation, facilities, and training considerations.

While not required to provide any more information than the minimum described earlier, you should consider addressing the following when drafting an LOR for a major weapon system:

Basic Identification Data

- Identify the type of response desired. The LOR must be specific as to what is expected from the implementing agency in response to the LOR. The LOR may request pricing and availability (P&A) data for planning purposes; this is not an offer to sell. A request for a Letter of Offer and Acceptance (LOA) will result in the IA providing an offer to sell defense articles and services. An amendment to an existing case which will result in the change to an implemented LOA may also be requested. If a lease of a defense article is desired, indicate this in the LOR to include the lease period. Be explicit about which product is requested in response to the LOR. For additional information click on the link to SAMM Section C5.2.
- If your country previously requested and received P&A information and now you want to ask for an LOA, your LOR should reference the FMS case identifier provided with the P&A. For example: "We request an LOA for items as defined in Price and Availability document BN- D-AAA provided by the U.S. Air Force letter number 11-AA on January 16, 2013."
- If requesting a lease, you must provide information about where the items will be used or based during the lease period and the duration of the requested lease. The U.S. response to a lease request is somewhat different than an LOA (See example in SAMM Figure C11.F6.). You will need to request a separate LOA (FMS case) or group of FMS cases to cover support costs for the items being leased, or you may specify in the lease LOR what existing FMS case will be used to cover support costs (spare parts, repair services, training, etc.). See more information on leases at SAMM Section C11.6.

- Specify who and what organization within your country is submitting the LOR (Army, Navy, Air Force, or other agency). Be as specific as possible, to include providing a name, phone number, mailing address and e-mail address. This is the person the Implementing Agency will contact if additional information is required.
- If any preliminary meetings with the Implementing Agency have taken place, you should include notes from those meetings with the LOR. If pricing was negotiated with a company before submitting the LOR, this information should be included in the LOR. If a price is negotiated after the LOR is submitted but prior to the USG obtaining the pricing for the items these negotiated prices and the name of the company should be provided to the IA so the price can be included in the final LOA.
- Identify any international competitions/solicitations related to the purchase, if any. The USG can respond to an international solicitation for defense equipment or services with an LOA. If your country has issued an international solicitation, request for information (RFI), or request for procurement (RFP), note this in the LOR and include copies of any documents so that we can ensure you receive a comprehensive response that meets all of the requirements specified in the solicitation, RFI, or RFP. More information on FMS and international competitions can be found at SAMM Section C4.3.1.
- Are you currently involved in commercial negotiations with potential U.S. suppliers/companies? As a matter of general policy, the USG does not provide FMS data if the purchasing country is involved in ongoing negotiations with a U.S. contractor for the same item (see SAMM Section C4.3.7.)
- Normally, the USG provides a date 60 days for you to review an LOA or LOA Amendment. We call this the Offer Expiration Date (OED) If, due to your government's internal structure or process, you need more than 60 days to review the document, you should include a comment to that effect in the LOR. Similarly, if you must have the LOA submitted to you by a specific date (perhaps to conform to your government's budgetary cycle), be sure to include that information also. Costs, delivery schedules, and other critical events are estimated based on your country accepting the LOA by the specified OED.

Capability needs

- Describe the type of equipment desired. Be as specific as possible. If you don't know or are not sure what you need, describe the operational/strategic requirement you are trying to meet so that the U.S. Implementing Agency can offer recommendations.
- Number of systems desired
- Configuration desired. Many end items have different options in both standard and non-standard configurations. For example, a truck may have several options to choose from; two or four wheel drive, standard or automatic transmission, with or without air conditioning, with or without gun mount, with or without ambulance litter fixtures, and others. These may all be standard options, but you must choose which configuration is needed. There may be other options available that are not part of the standard U.S. configuration. Standard versions are usually less expensive, easier to support, and easier to upgrade or modify.
- Where you expect to base those systems and where you expect their operational areas will be.
- Interoperability requirements. What other existing national systems must the items you are purchasing be interoperable with? Do you wish your systems to be interoperable with the United States or with another nation?
- The concept of operation and operational tempo for the equipment (how will you employ them, how often will they be used, how long will the missions be, and under what sorts of environmental conditions?)
- The operational or strategic effect your country would like to achieve with this equipment

- Reliability, maintainability, and availability requirements. This information will influence many things, including the recommended number of systems and accompanying training and support package.
- Required delivery dates for capability (describe when and how many you need for initial training, for an Initial Operational Capability (IOC), and for Full Operational Capability (FOC). This information can affect the production schedule and cost of the total package. If no specific timeline is given, the implementing agency will select the option with the lowest cost and most convenient delivery timeline when writing the LOA.

Affordability

- What is your country's budget for this program?
- What is the funding source (your country's national funds, U.S. Foreign Military Financing (FMF), an existing Memorandum of Agreement (MOA) or Memorandum of Understanding (MOU) with the United States)?
- Are there any special payment requirements you have? Information on the required initial deposit and future payment schedule is included with the LOA the U.S. sends you. The initial deposit is required at the time your country's approval authority accepts the case. If your country's budgeting and approval process make it necessary, you can indicate in the LOR a maximum initial deposit and the appropriate timing for the payment.
- Payment schedules normally require quarterly payments to DFAS in advance of estimated deliveries or anticipated expenditures, such as those for progress payments to the contractor. If you have a specific budget that must be adhered to, it may be feasible to modify the payment schedule - as long as it still meets the financial requirements of the FMS case.
- The FMS system does allow for some pricing waivers. Two common examples are: non-recurring costs associated with the purchase of Major Defense Equipment (MDE) and waiver of the contract administrative surcharge. See SAMM Section C9.6. for additional information on waivers and discuss them with the Implementing Agency to determine whether your country is eligible. If pricing waivers are not requested in the LOR, LOA pricing will include these costs if applicable.

Acquisition

- Will this capability be acquired entirely via FMS or by a combination of FMS and DCS?
- Are there any special considerations related to the acquisition approach for this capability? Is there anything about the capability needed, the timeline it is needed within, and its affordability that will require a special approach, such as incremental acquisition or a lease as a gap-filler?
- **Noncompetitive procurement.** To the greatest extent possible, the USG prefers to procure items under full and open competition. However, if your country already has a specific type of equipment made by a certain manufacturer, you may wish to procure future items from the same manufacturer to ensure commonality of spare parts. Or your country may, for other reasons, decided to use a particular U.S. manufacturer, or limit consideration to a certain group of contractors. We call these "Sole Source" requests and they must be submitted to us in writing - preferably in the LOR since the decision to procure Sole Source may significantly impact the cost and schedule we provide in the LOA. The sole source request must comply with the criteria in SAMM Section C6.3.4., and should be submitted with the LOR.

Logistics

- What, if any, are your existing logistics capabilities related to the proposed sale (facilities, support equipment, trained personnel, etc.).

- Maintenance concept. Do you plan to conduct maintenance within your country at the organizational, intermediate, and depot level? The answer has important implications for the spare parts and support package that comes with the case. Will you use your own maintenance and supply resources or do you plan to use U.S. contracted resources or those of another country?
- Length of spares/repairs support. In your LOR, specify the number of years/months you would like to receive spare parts support for the major item you are purchasing. The Implementing Agency will assure that at least one year, and usually two years, of spare parts are included in the LOA.
- Support equipment. The Implementing Agency will include all of the necessary support equipment to test, repair, and maintain major end items you requested. If your country already has the necessary support equipment, then include that information in the LOR.
- Country requested material handling equipment (MHE)
- Facilities (construction). Will your country need additional facilities (or to modify existing facilities) to house, support, and maintain the new equipment? Do current facilities meet the expected operational and support requirements? For example, is the runway at the air base where new aircraft will be delivered long enough and strong enough for them? Also, if your country is obligated to provide a certain level of security for any sensitive U.S. items purchased - such as night vision devices - it may be necessary for you to construct or upgrade storage facilities.

Country Data Requirements

- Does your country require any additional data beyond that needed for standard operation and maintenance? If so, you should specify this in your LOR.
- Publications. The Implementing Agency will ensure the LOA includes publications needed for the end items and for the support systems in the LOA. These publications will be provided in English. These are considered standard publications. Non-standard publications, such as those that are specially tailored or translated into another language, should be requested in the LOR.

Training

- Will your country require training to operate or support the end items?
- Do you prefer to conduct training in your country or in the United States?
- Do you have any preferences or restrictions on whether the training is provided by the U.S. Department of Defense, by contractors, or a combination of the two?
- Do you already have training devices (such as simulators)?
- English Language Training (ELT). Most U.S.-provided training is conducted in English. Therefore, the personnel your country sends to attend training will need a certain level of English comprehension before they can begin. If needed, the U.S. can provide English language training in your country or at the Defense Language Institute's English Language Training Center in Texas. If ELT is a consideration for your purchase, provide a description of your current capabilities, your needs, and preferences with regard to ELT delivery.

Transportation

- Transportation of LOA material can be accomplished by your government, by a freight forwarder your government employs, or by the USG using the Defense Transportation System (DTS). Your LOR should include delivery preferences for the various types of material (major items, spares, munitions, publications), as well as any classified or hazardous materials. If you will use a freight forwarder, the LOR should identify the company and the type of freight it is cleared to handle. The

Defense Institute for Security Assistance Management (DISAM) publishes a Freight Forwarder Selection Guide that can be found at the Publications tab of the DISAM website.

- Staging Services. If requested in the LOR, the USG can arrange for consolidation of spare/repair parts or support equipment at a staging area for your pickup or for other dedicated transport to your country. Otherwise, the most common approach is for the USG to ship these items to your freight forwarder where they are consolidated pending onward shipment to your country.
- Insurance. Your country must self-insure FMS shipments or obtain commercial insurance without any right of claim against the United States. This includes for returns. In exceptional situations, if requested in the LOR, an Implementing Agency may obtain insurance and the cost of the insurance will be billed as a separate line item on the Letter of Offer and Acceptance.
- SAMM Chapter 7 explains FMS transportation in detail.

Program Development and Management

- Do you anticipate the need for U.S. assistance with defining your requirements and/or conducting a site survey (note: depending upon the circumstances, the Implementing Agency may itself later recommend joint requirements definition meetings and/or site surveys in order to complete the LOA)?
- Liaison Office. If your country would like to establish a Foreign Liaison Office in the United States (at the manufacturing plant or other key location), or have the USG establish a U.S. Field Office in your country to assist with program management, you should specify this in the LOR.
- Special logistical or financial reports. Special reports are those reports not available to the customer through the Security Cooperation Information Portal (SCIP). Examples are the LOA's supporting Manpower and Travel Data Worksheet (MTDS), the Defense Security Assistance Management System's (DSAMS's) Current Implemented Case Report, and LOA Line Item Pricing Calculations. Special reports provided by the Implementing Agency are above the Standard Level of Service so may incur additional costs. SAMM Table C9.T2. provides DSCA guidelines on Standard Level of Service.

Other Requests

- **Warranties.** The Implementing Agency obtains the same warranties for FMS as it does for itself at no additional cost (SAMM Section C6.3.8.). These warranties are exercised within the Supply Discrepancy Report (SDR) process and do not require any special notation by you in the LOR. However, if your country requires any additional performance warranties, you should indicate so in the LOR. The Implementing Agency will negotiate these warranties with the contractor and will include any additional costs in the LOA.
- **Special Contract Terms.** Identify any special contract terms your country may require. Depending upon the situation and the type of contract being used, the USG may or may not be able to accommodate a given request, but identifying the requirement early, in the LOR, will provide the U.S. program manager and contracting officer the maximum amount of time to determine whether your country's request is feasible and, if not, to identify potential alternatives for meeting your needs.
- Specify any desire for enhanced visibility and/or participation in the LOA development process. You should be aware that increased participation in the LOA development could slow the process, lengthen the time it takes the USG to offer your country an LOA, and increase costs.
- **Offsets.** The DoD may not enter into or commit U.S. firms to any offset agreement. Responsibility for negotiating offset arrangements and satisfying all related commitments resides with the U.S. firm

involved. The USG will not include offset arrangements in an LOA. However, the U.S. contractor may request offset costs be included as part of the line item(s) unit cost in P&A data and in the estimated prices quoted in an LOA. You can learn more about offsets at SAMM Section C3.9.1.

Appendix 2 - How to Obtain Access to the Security Cooperation Information Portal (SCIP)

If you would like a SCIP account, you should first check to see if your country already has access to SCIP. If so, someone in the appropriate organization within your Ministry of Defense or, in some cases, someone at your embassy in the U.S., will have been designated a "SCIP Token Administrator." We also call these "host nation token administrators" or "HNTA". Your country's SCIP Token Administrator can provide you with a SCIP token. You can then register on-line at https://www.scportal.us.

- At the very top of the page you can click on "Registration Info" which will bring up another page.
- On the lower right side of that page click on "SCIP Registration Form". During registration, you will use a token number from one of your tokens so that the SCIP team at the Defense Security Assistance Development Center (DSADC) can activate and associate that token number to your SCIP account.
- If you are confused by anything in the form, you can request clarification/assistance from the SCIP Help Desk by e-mailing SCIPHelp@dsadc.dsca.mil.
- The registration form is not short and, once you fill it out, you will need to print it, and then either scan it and send it to the SCIP Help Desk as an e-mail attachment or fax it to them at (717) 605-9082.

If your country does not yet have a SCIP Token Administrator, you can designate one, obtain tokens, and then begin creating SCIP accounts. Here's what you will need to do:

1. Fill out a letter to designate someone within your government a SCIP Token Administrator (click here to see a template).
2. Send the signed letter as an e-mail attachment to the SCIP Help Desk at SCIPHelp@dsadc.dsca.mil. In the text of the e-mail, specify the number of tokens you think you need, and provide an address where you would like the tokens sent. The Defense Security Assistance Development Center (DSADC) will send the token(s) to that address. Once you receive the tokens, you will need to inform DSADC. They will insert instructions for contacting them in the package with the tokens and in an e-mail to you.
3. Once you have the tokens, you can fill out a SCIP Registration form on-line at https://www.scportal.us. At the very top of the page you can click on "Registration Info" which will bring up another page. On the lower right side of that page click on "SCIP Registration Form". During registration, you will use a token number from one of your tokens so that the SCIP team at the Defense Security Assistance Development Center (DSADC) can activate and associate that token number to your SCIP account. If you are confused by anything in the form, you can request clarification/assistance from the SCIP Help Desk by e-mailing SCIPHelp@dsadc.dsca.mil. The registration form is not short and, once you fill it out, you will need to print it, and then either scan it and send it to the SCIP Help Desk (SCIPHelp@dsadc.dsca.mil) as an e-mail attachment or fax it to them at (717) 605-9082. If you have any questions about the form you can ask the SCIP Help staff for assistance at SCIPHelp@dsadc.dsca.mil.

Template for Designating SCIP Token Administrators

-Your Country's Official Letterhead-

GOVERNMENT OF _____

Address:_____

SCIP Access Administration Team
Defense Security Assistance Development Center (DSADC)
5450 Carlisle Pike
Building 107n
Mechanicsburg, Pa. 17055
Fax Number: Commercial: (717) 605-9082

SUBJECT: Designation of Host Nation Token Administrator and Alternate

1. The personnel listed below have been designated by the Government of _____ to act as Token Administrator and Alternate Token Administrator for the Security Cooperation Information Portal.

2. Should you have any additional questions, please contact (printed name, title, phone number, fax number, email, and address of the Designating Official)

Signature of the Designating Official

Signature Block of the Designating Official

1. Token Administrator:
    Name (Printed)
    Title
    Telephone Number
    Fax Number
    Address
    Email Address
    Signature

2. Alternate Token Administrator:
    Name (Printed)
    Title
    Telephone Number
    Fax Number
    Address
    Email Address
    Signature